ideals®
EASTER ISSUE

Dear Reader:

Your response to *Fireside Ideals* was most gratifying. We are pleased that you have enjoyed our new features, the Ideals Best-Loved Poets and Ideals Pages from the Past. In this issue we are featuring Garnett Ann Schultz and selected pages from *Easter Ideals*, 1953, along with colorful pictures of delicate wild flowers, majestic scenery and many pages of enriching verse. You will also enjoy the inspiring paintings depicting this Holy Easter season.

We hope that you will continue to send the names and addresses of your friends to us (c/o Dept. Ed.) so that we may send them our latest brochure featuring Ideals books and products. Also, we are always interested in hearing your thoughts on what you would like to see in Ideals magazine. We welcome *your* suggestions!

We wish you all a very joyful Easter season.

Sincerely,

Ralph Luedtke
Managing Editor

Managing Editor, Ralph Luedtke
Associate Editor, Robin Lee Dennison
Photographic Editor, Gerald Koser
Production Editor, Stuart L. Zyduck

It Must Be Spring

There is a mildness in the air . . . A softness
in the soil . . . And there is less of weariness . . .
In struggle and in toil . . . The sun is somewhat
warmer now . . . The sky a brighter blue . . .
And something seems to tell the heart . . . That
life is fresh and new . . . It must be time for
spring again . . . And time to look around . . .
For greener grass and flowers fair . . . To
decorate the ground . . . The snow and ice
have disappeared . . . Where now the rivers
flow . . . And fertile fields are stirring in . . .
Their eagerness to grow . . . The soul is filled
with faith and hope . . . And joy in everything
. . . It must be time to live again . . . It must be
really spring.

James J. Metcalfe

IDEALS—Vol. 35, No. 2—March 1978. Published bimonthly by IDEALS PUBLISHING CORPORATION, 11315 Watertown Plank Road,
Milwaukee, Wis. 53226. Second-class postage paid at Milwaukee, Wisconsin. © 1978 by IDEALS PUBLISHING CORPORATION.
All rights reserved. Title IDEALS registered U.S. Patent Office.

ONE YEAR SUBSCRIPTION—six consecutive issues as published—only $10.00
TWO YEAR SUBSCRIPTION—twelve consecutive issues as published—only $17.00
SINGLE ISSUES—only $2.50

*Photo opposite
Hampfler Studios*

ISBN 0-89542-313-8

JAY KILLIAN

The year holds one moment, which may last for a week, when tree and bush and vine are on the breathless verge of leafing out. It is then that one can stand on a hilltop and look across the valley and see the scarlet and orange maple blossoms like a touch of pastel crayon across the treetops.

I saw such a generalization today and I knew that breathless moment is here. Then I began to look for particulars. The pear tree beside the garden is dressed in green lace, its leaves no larger than my little fingernail. The lilacs are tufted at their stem-ends, each twin leaf cluster tipped with faint brownish purple and not a leaf among them as big as a squirrel's ear. The wild raspberries beside the river have scarlet tassels not half an inch long, each tassel an unfolding group of leaves whose form can be faintly seen. The early apple trees have silver gray nubs at their twig tips; when I drew down a branch to look I could see each nub as a young leaf cluster emerging from the bud, each leaf the size of a ladybird's wing and each red-tipped as though blushing. The bridal-wreath bush is green at every joint with little green rosebud leaves.

These things are here now, this instant. Even an hour from now all will be changed. Tomorrow it will be still different. This is the trembling moment when life stands between bud and leaf, promise and achievement. A new world is in the making on these old, old hills. I am an observer while Creation is taking place.

Hal Borland

Easter

Against a sky of blue and gray,
The dawn of Easter greets the day;
The lilies raise their heads up high
To kiss the early morning sky.

In bright array upon the hills,
The tulips and the daffodils,
With flaming colors warm and fair,
Tell us God is everywhere.

And that is why the Easter birth
Brings hope and peace across the earth;
For all things whisper God is true
As Easter morning comes to view.

Patricia Emme

Joy

Already the slim crocus stirs the snow,
And soon yon blanched fields will bloom again

With nodding cowslips for some lad to mow;
For with the first warm kisses of the rain,

The winter's icy sorrow breaks to tears
And the brown thrushes mate, and with bright eyes the rabbit peers

From the dark warren where the fir cones lie,
And treads one snowdrop under foot, and runs

Over the mossy knoll, and blackbirds fly
Across our path at evening, and the suns

Stay longer with us: ah, how good to see
Grass-girdled Spring in all her joy of laughing greenery!

Oscar Wilde

It's Easter Again

It's the time of renewal beginning again:
Great clumps of violets purple the lane.

There's a change in the landscape wherever you look.
The duck takes her brood for a swim in the brook.

Bottom lands bloom with bright buttercups
While a new mother romps with her frisky young pups.

High on the bluff where the winds are still cold,
The thoroughbred nuzzles her long-legged foal.

The chanticleer tells of some sweet baby chicks
Who are fretting the hen with their mischievous tricks.

A carpet of grass has covered the lawn—
The woodlands boast of a white-spotted fawn.

Everything's fresh with the softness of down,
Even the willow wears a new fuzzy gown.

The world is alive with the newness of things:
It's Easter again and the grateful heart sings.

Alice Leedy Mason

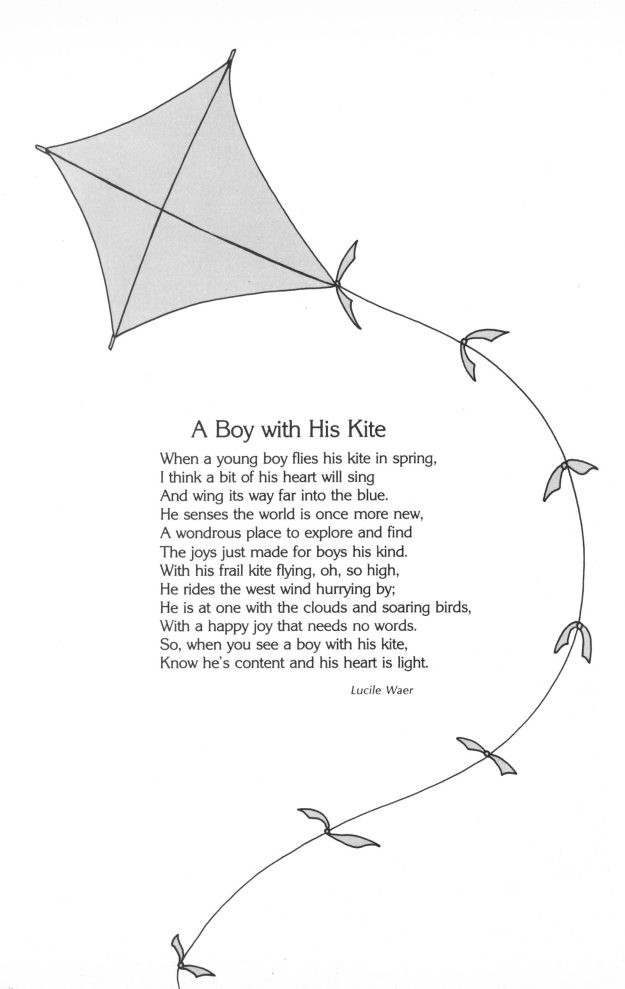

A Boy with His Kite

When a young boy flies his kite in spring,
I think a bit of his heart will sing
And wing its way far into the blue.
He senses the world is once more new,
A wondrous place to explore and find
The joys just made for boys his kind.
With his frail kite flying, oh, so high,
He rides the west wind hurrying by;
He is at one with the clouds and soaring birds,
With a happy joy that needs no words.
So, when you see a boy with his kite,
Know he's content and his heart is light.

Lucile Waer

The imaginative sculpturing of greenery has intrigued gardeners ever since the days of the Greeks and Romans. In those days wealthy citizens surrounded their country villas with pleasure gardens in which many plants were pruned and clipped into whimsical and architectural forms.

Whether the Romans carried the tradition of topiary with them to England is not known, but the art of topiary—the training, pruning, and clipping of plants to create unusual shapes—reached its zenith in seventeenth- and eighteenth-century England. The art was perfected also in France and Holland during those years, where palaces and castles were surrounded with pleasure gardens accented and decorated with topiary forms. Some of these ancient gardens are still intact, still trimmed and carefully manicured, and still forming an elaborate setting for these historic buildings.

The colonists came to America with memories of pruned hedges and shaped plants; and as their own gardens became established and their way of life took on a more leisurely pattern, they began to create topiary figures to enhance their own surroundings. In the South today you can see topiary gardens that were established two hundred years ago.

Topiary is still a popular form of ornamental gardening; and although many kinds of plants can be used, boxwood is probably the favorite. It takes kindly to pruning, its small-leaved foliage is thick and full, and it is a very long-lived plant. One disadvantage is that it is not winter hardy in the North. Boxwood should be pruned in early spring, before new growth begins.

Japanese yew is another favorite for topiary, popular for its hardiness and its fine texture. It responds well to clipping and shaping, but it is a slow grower and will not fill in as quickly as some others. Yew should be clipped in midsummer.

The Ancien

Right: Longwood Gardens, Kennett Square, Pennsylvania. Below: Green Animals Gardens, Portsmouth, Rhode Island.

Privet, traditionally a hedge plant, is hardy, inexpensive, and fast growing, and it makes a fine topiary; but it is not evergreen and so loses its charm during cold months.

Other plants often used are hemlock, juniper, and euonymus (Euonymus japonica), which can be shaped easily but is not hardy in the North. Many vines and some smaller trees, too, are used in topiary. In general, none should be pruned in late fall as freezing weather might cause damage.

Many of the architectural topiary forms—pyramids, globes, obelisks, spirals—require sizeable shrubs; but today's electric

Art of Topiary

There are many famous topiary gardens both here and abroad—for instance, the maze at Hampton Court, the palace of Henry VIII near London, with its initials "W" and "M" carved in it in honor of William and Mary; its counterpart, the holly maze in the garden of the Governor's Palace at Williamsburg, Virginia, can be admired from the nearby "mount." At Hidecote Manor in Gloucestershire, England, you can see the so-called "stilts" topiary, a double row of hornbeam trees whose bare trunks form an alley of columns topped by square-shaped clipped foliage; at Compton Wynyates in Warwickshire the topiary gardens of the ancient castle still stand like sentinels guarding the path from meadow to moat. And, of course, in France, the most famous of all on the continent, are the topiaries of the extensive gardens at Versailles Palace, designed by the garden architect LeNotre and built for King Louis XIV.

There are excellent American topiary gardens. At Portsmouth, Rhode Island, near Newport, is Green Animals Topiary Gardens, open to visitors daily from mid-June to the end of September. This is one of the best known, although perhaps not the most beautiful, of America's topiary collections. Almost a hundred animals of every size and variety are carved out of greenery.

Longwood Gardens, Kennett Square, Pennsylvania, has a fine collection; traditional topiaries including hedges, pyramids, and other architectural forms accent its lawns and border the pathways. It is open daily for visitors all year.

At Pleasant Valley Farm in Harford County, Maryland, just outside of Baltimore, is the Harvey Ladew Topiary Gardens. These green creations tell the story of the originator's lifetime interest in the hunt, for running across a lawn is a topiary fox, forever pursued by a pack of hunting hounds, all followed by a life-sized topiary horse and rider. It is open on weekends from May through October.

Margaret Perry

pruning shears make the task easier than it used to be. More complicated figures, such as birds and animals, are usually supported by wire on which the plants are trained. Hardware cloth or chicken wire is bent into the desired shape, filled with sphagnum moss, and the young plants inserted into the moss, which should be kept constantly moist until the plants take hold.

A year or so after the topiary is started—depending on what kind of plant is used—the form will begin to take on its proper shape, helped by pruning and clipping. After the topiary has become well established, it needs only two or three trimmings a year to keep it looking its best.

Reprinted from the April, 1977 issue of Early American Life Magazine with permission from the publisher.

GARDENER'S CREED

I believe in good brown earth, sun and seed and soil.
Rest is sweetest when it comes after happy toil . . . I
believe in miracles, bud and leaf and fruit—springing
into loveliness from the hidden root.

I believe that God who made rose and bird and bee—
wanted us to make His world beautiful to see—Meant
us to be gardeners, making green things grow. I
believe we do His work when we plant and sow.

I believe that He whose Hand fashioned Eden's
bowers—put into the heart of man love of trees and
flowers . . . That is why a garden gives us blessings
manifold—health and healing and contentment, peace
and joys untold.

Patience Strong

Photo Media Ltd.

"I believe we do His work

when we plant and sow."

Garnett Ann Schultz

Perhaps more than any other poet, Garnett Ann Schultz is associated with Ideals—an association which has extended more than twenty-seven years and over three hundred poems. Garnett Ann has lived all her life in the family home in southwest Pennsylvania. Today the land around the house is a great sloping lawn, but her childhood memories are of the farm her father worked "for his amazement or amusement." Those days were filled with the smell of newly mown hay and the chores and joys of country living. Today, however, Garnett Ann has retired from her secretarial job at U.S. Steel and leads a busy life caring for her sister, corresponding with the elderly as well as college students, teaching children to play the piano and, of course, writing poetry. She believes that her greatest joy and constant goal is to impart happiness to others. An optimist still, her poetry reflects this desire and ability to see the good in the world and dispense it to others. She wrote, many years ago, "It seems I never quite outgrew / Those happy circus days I knew." May she outgrow them never. On these two pages are selections of her poetry.

I Found a Road

I found a road—a country road
Where hills reach to the sky,
With grass grown tall and tiny streams
And little birds that fly;
Across the way of hopes and dreams
All mellowed by the years,
Where friendly folks will shake your hand
And wipe away life's fears.

I found a road—all lined with trees
And white clouds far above,
No thought of haste, no hurry here
But moments filled with love;
A springtime day—where flowers bloom,
A wide expanse so grand,
Beneath the heavens bright and free
God's bit of wondrous land.

Do keep the little country ways,
The beauties ever there,
In summer's sun or winter's snow
Oh, such a worthwhile share,
Where feet might walk in quiet faith
And hearts can lose life's load,
Within the soul of nature's best
Was where I found a road.

Easter Is

Easter is a happy time
Of lovely budding trees,
It's colored eggs and deep blue skies,
A tender springtime breeze,
It's little girls all dressed in style,
A robin on the wing;
It's baby chicks so fluffy soft,
And sunshine of the spring.

Easter is a blessed time:
It's prayers that fill our heart,
A something rich and beautiful
Believing can impart;
It's big wide eyes on Easter morn,
Oh, such a goodly share,
To know that in the still of night
Our bunny friend was there.

Easter is a world of joy,
A world of hope to keep,
To live and grow within His arms,
A chance to sow and reap;
It's tender smiles and loving friends,
A shower—then the sun;
It's winter's end and spring's rebirth
With faith for everyone.

I Think of These

I think of these:
The sky so blue,
The sun's bright rays,
The raindrops too,
The valleys fair,
The hills that climb,
A rainbow bright
That God made mine.

I think of joys
In faith unseen,
The trees of gold,
The snowflakes gleam,
The stars of wonder,
Moonlight's glow,
The mountains tall,
The world below.

I think of love,
A dream to share,
A bit of hope,
A courage rare,
The troubled hours
When cares are mine,
The peaceful moments,
Still sublime.

I often pause
In springtime hours,
To hold the beauty
Of God's flowers,
The birds on wing,
The outstretched trees,
With humble heart
I think of these.

Nature Rules

Nature holds beauty
And all of it free;
The bright touch of splendor,
The wide-spreading tree,
Spectacular—wondrous,
The warm golden sun;
Do open your heart, dear,
And find every one.

The universe beckons
One glorious dream,
So filled with its music,
Revelation supreme;
From season to season,
From day unto day,
Something new to delight us
And brighten our way.

The fragrance of pine wood,
The world fresh and new,
Touched by the sparkle
Of dawning's first dew;
A star in the heavens
Exploring the sky,
A sunbeam through treetops,
A moonbeam on high.

Nature is smiling
In each living thing;
In raindrops and storm clouds,
The outdoors is king;
A peace and contentment,
Rich beauty so fair,
The whole world is God's mansion;
For nature rules there.

Message of Spring

I know a place where violets bring
Their sweet perfume in early spring . . .

Where Dutchman's Breeches hang arow,
Mid lacy leaves their garments blow.

In ivory-white, May blossoms gleam
And peep from parasols of green.

From mottled leaves, trout lilies glance,
While buttercups and windflowers dance.

Here jaunty Jack-in-pulpits preach,
Neath sheltering arms of spreading beech.

The wind's soft music fills the air,
A wood thrush trills in concert rare.

In sweet simplicity they bring
Their tribute to God's world of spring

And glorify life's ordered plan
Of truth and beauty, hope, to man.

E. M. Koopman

Photo opposite
JACK-IN-THE-PULPIT
Arnout Hyde, Jr.

from the editor's scrapbook

Easter is an awakening of every living thing. A time when soul and spirits rise, as heaven receives its King.

Olive Dunkelberger

Come out, come out across the hills!
The golden blossoms call.

Sara Hamilton Birchall

My heart sings with the robins in the rain,
For I remember it is Easter morn,
And life and love and peace are all newborn,
And joy has triumphed over loss and pain.

Alice Freeman Palmer

Be still, and know that I am God.

Psalm 46:10

Spring has come when you can put your foot on three daisies at once.

Author Unknown

The brightest and most enduring flowers along the waysides of life are smiles, the sparkle of the eye, loving words, little acts of kindness . . . they never wholly fade from memory. Often after years they are brighter than on the day we first beheld them.

Edgar Linton

Blessed are they that hear the word of God and keep it.

Luke 11:28

Kindness in words creates confidence,
Kindness in thinking creates profoundness,
Kindness in giving creates love.

Lao-Tse

I am glad that in the springtime of
life there were those who planted
the flowers of love in my heart
instead of thistles.

Robert Louis Stevenson

Close to my heart I fold each lovely thing
the sweet day yields; and not disconsolate
with calm impatience of the woods, I wait
for leaf and blossom, when God gives us
spring.

John Greenleaf Whittier

Art and blue heaven,
April and God's larks,
Green reeds and
Sky-scattering river.
A stately music—
Enter, God!

Robert Louis Stevenson

Flowers are the poetry of earth, as
stars are the poetry of heaven.

Author Unknown

All that I have seen teaches me to
trust the Creator for what I have
not seen.

Author Unkown

Be like the bird, halting in his flight
Awhile in boughs so light,
Feels them give way beneath him
    and yet sings
Knowing that he hath wings.

Victor Hugo

Easter
ISSUE
ideals

Ideals' Pages from the Past

On the following four pages we are presenting a selection from Easter Ideals 1953.

It's Easter

Vivian Volk

The robin's song is gayer,
Soft and sweet as a prayer.
The grass seems a bit more green,
With more crocuses on the scene.
The chapel bells softer ring,
While choristers sweeter sing.
The sun seems friendlier, too;
Heaven dons a brighter blue.

Folks all wear a happy smile,
While dressed in the newest style —
What occasion or reason,
Or is it just the season?
Listen close, your heart will say,
"Hope reborn — it's Easter Day."

One Easter Long Ago

Mrs. Roy L. Peifer

When I was but a little miss,
   And you a sturdy boy,
We planned one Eastertime to fill
   Our mother's heart with joy.
We wanted to surprise her;
   We yearned to make her glad;
So we saved up all our money —
   Every penny that we had.

And we'd creep away to count it,
   In the attic dim and cool,
Or to add some hoarded coppers
   To that precious little pool.
Then we'd whisper, plan and giggle
   In our innocence and bliss —
When you were but a sturdy boy,
   And I a little miss.

We wished to buy a flower —
   A fragrant lily tall —
But the pile grew, O, so slowly!
   Though we scrimped and saved it all.
And then one sunny morning
   While we planned and whispered there,
We heard a telltale little squeak
   Upon the attic stair.

We thought that Mother'd heard us!
We wondered if she had —
But when the smiling face appeared,
We saw that it was Dad.
His eyes were bright and happy,
And we knew he must have heard.
But he reached into his pocket
And he never said a word.

Then early Easter morning
  We went to Mother's bed
With our sacrificial offering —
  A pot of tulips red.
Since then has many a springtime passed;
  And many a lovelier bloom
Has found its way on Easter day
  To brighten Mother's room.

But none was ever loved so much —
  Indeed, none seemed so fine —
As that first simple blossom
  On that long gone Easter time.
Then, with lots of love and pennies,
  A little lass and lad
Bought an Easter flower for Mother —
  With a little help from Dad!

Blossoms on the Bough

A bright young breeze is bearing
The scent of petals now,
Where all the sky above me
Is wreathed in apple boughs.

The small brown buds of springtime
Are bursting one by one,
And whiter grows the hillside
With blossoms in the sun.

I love each precious moment
Of my rendezvous with spring,
When birds of every feather
Find happy cause to sing.

Their fluted notes of gladness
Swell from every bough,
Where bright bouquets are weaving
A sky of petaled clouds.

The breeze is sweet with blossoms
And the air is filled with song;
How can I leave the hillside
Where all of April throngs?

Each moment brings its blessing
As boughs around me sigh
And lift their lacy silhouettes
Against the azure sky.

'Tis only God could fashion
The beauty of it all;
The miracle of springtime,
And the blossoms on the bough.

Joy Belle Burgess

Christ the Lord Is Risen Today

CHARLES WESLEY

FROM LYRA DAVIDICA

Christ the Lord is risen to-day, Al — le - lu - ia!

Sons of men and an - gels say, Al — le - lu - ia!

Raise your joys and tri - umphs high, Al — le - lu - ia!

Sing, ye heavens, and earth re - ply, Al — le - lu - ia! Amen

Charles Wesley

Charles Wesley (1707-1788), brother to the great John Wesley, founder of Methodism, is often described as the younger and "lesser" Wesley. Charles is, however, important in his own right. This younger Wesley wrote the lyrics for 6,500 hymns and changed the course of hymnody.

Wesley's first hymnal, *Hymns and Sacred Poems*, was published in 1739. This volume marked the beginning of Wesley's use of hymns to aid in his and his brother's preaching. Included in this 1739 publication is the stirring and beloved "Christ the Lord Is Risen Today." This poem reflects the musical legacy of Charles Wesley: the use of literary convention in hymns.

Prior to Wesley, church congregations were, for the most part, limited to the metrical psalm which only gradually gave way to the hymn psalm. Charles Wesley, however, introduced a variety of meters in his poems and raised the quality of the lyric to that of poetic literature. Wesley changed the religious song from a somewhat somber tone to a joyful and moving praise to God.

With such a prolific outpouring from his pen, all of Wesley's hymns have not retained their popularity. Many, however, remain popular two hundred years after they were composed. For instance, those such as "Christ the Lord Is Risen Today," "Hark! The Herald Angels Sing," and "Love Divine, All Love Excelling" are familiar to many congregations.

In 1740, Wesley penned the prayerful lyrics: "O for a thousand tongues to sing My great Redeemer's praise. My gracious Master and my God, Assist me to proclaim, To spread through all the earth abroad the honors of thy name." That petition was answered, and we are richer for it.

Patricia Pingry

Lives again our glorious King, Alleluia!
Where, O death, is now thy sting? Alleluia!
Once He died, our souls to save, Alleluia!
Where's thy victory, boasting grave? Alleluia!

Love's redeeming work is done, Alleluia!
Fought the fight, the battle won, Alleluia!
Death in vain forbids Him rise, Alleluia!
Christ hath opened Paradise, Alleluia!

Soar we now where Christ has led, Alleluia!
Following our exalted Head, Alleluia!
Made like Him, like Him we rise, Alleluia!
Ours the cross, the grave, the skies, Alleluia!

Springtime in the Rockies

Springtime has come to the mountains,
    Under the arch of the sky;
Streams wear sun-glinted diamonds,
    Clouds float lazily by.

Little trails wind ever upward;
    Wild flowers blossom again.
Columbine, violets and crocus
    Welcome the dew and the rain.

Pine trees grow so majestic;
    Green leaves cover the ground.
The view from the top of a mountain
    Is nothing less than profound!

The lake, like a clear crystal mirror,
    Reflects the sky overhead.
Moss creeps over the boulders,
    Smooth as a new featherbed.

Springtime's the loveliest of seasons,
    Soft as the touch of a cloud.
Sweet is the music of mountains—
    Only God's praises allowed.

                    Alice Leedy Mason

Blood Root

Alpha Photo Associates

DAWN

Dawn is the fountainhead of light, hope and love; at dawn Nature awakes, and all creatures, roused from sleep and strengthened, assemble anew. The night sprinkles the path of dawn with dew; at dawn the flowers bud, that the sun may find everything adorned.

Spring Beauty

The mute silence of the night breaks; pleasant and merry harmonies begin. The birds sing cheerfully, cool breezes whisper through the thick wood, a festive spirit reigns over hill and dale and zephyrs caress the calm sea. Mothers, wake your children, that they may see the dawn and be kissed by her first ray.

Bird's Foot Violets

At dawn I look upon nature
and a fresh vitality seems to be
filling mountains, hills,
woods and fields. I observe
manifold beauties, and my mind
is at ease when I see them.
When I perceive these miracles,
I am filled with the spirit
that created them.

Ljudevit Vulicevic

C. D. Barton

The Easter Story

Then came the day of unleavened bread, when the passover must be killed. And he sent Peter and John, saying, Go and prepare us the passover, that we may eat. And they said unto him, Where wilt thou that we prepare? And he said unto them, Behold, when ye are entered into the city, there shall a man meet you, bearing a pitcher of water; follow him into the house where he entereth in. And ye shall say unto the goodman of the house, The Master saith unto thee, Where is the guest chamber, where I shall eat the passover with my disciples? And he shall show you a large upper room furnished: there make ready. And they went, and found as he had said unto them: and they made ready the passover.

And when the hour was come, he sat down, and the twelve apostles with him. And he said unto them, With desire I have desired to eat this passover with you before I suffer: For I say unto you, I will not any more eat thereof, until it be fulfilled in the kingdom of God. And he took the cup, and gave thanks, and said, Take this, and divide it among yourselves: For I say unto you, I will not drink of the fruit of the vine, until the kingdom of God shall come.

And he took bread, and gave thanks, and brake it, and gave unto them, saying, This is my body which is given for you: this do in remembrance of me. Likewise also the cup after supper, saying, This cup is the new testament in my blood, which is shed for you.

Luke 22:7-20

*Behold the hour is at hand, and the Son of man is betrayed into
the hands of sinners.*

Then cometh Jesus with them unto a place called Gethse-
mane, and saith unto the disciples, Sit ye here, while I go and
pray yonder . . . And he went a little further, and fell on his
face, and prayed, saying O my Father, if it be possible, let this cup
pass from me: nevertheless, not as I will, but as thou wilt . . . Then
cometh he to his disciples and saith unto them, Sleep on now, and
take your rest: behold the hour is at hand, and the Son of man is
betrayed into the hands of sinners. Rise, let us be going: behold, he
is at hand that doth betray me.

And while he yet spake, lo, Judas, one of the twelve, came and
with him a great multitude with swords and staves, from the chief
priests and elders of the people. Now he that betrayed him gave
them a sign, saying, Whomsoever I shall kiss, that same is he; hold
him fast. And forthwith he came to Jesus, and said, Hail, Master; and
kissed him. And Jesus said unto him, Friend, wherefore art thou
come? Then came they, and laid hands on Jesus, and took him.
And, behold, one of them which were with Jesus stretched out his
hand, and drew his sword, and struck a servant of the high priest,
and smote off his ear. Then said Jesus unto him, Put up again thy
sword into his place: for all they that take the sword shall perish
with the sword. Thinkest thou that I cannot now pray to my Father,
and he shall presently give me more than twelve legions of angels?
But how then shall the Scriptures be fulfilled, that thus it must be?

Matt. 26:36, 39, 45-54

*When Pilate saw that he could prevail nothing . . . he took
water, and washed his hands.*

And the whole multitude of them arose, and led him unto
Pilate, and they began to accuse him, saying, We found this
fellow perverting the nation, and forbidding to give tribute
to Caesar, saying that he himself is Christ a king. And Pilate asked
him, saying, Art thou the King of Jews? And he answered him and
said, Thou sayest it. Then said Pilate to the chief priests and to the
people, I find no fault in this man. And they were the more fierce,
saying, He stirreth up the people . . .

And Pilate, when he had called together the chief priests and the
rulers and the people, Said unto them, Ye have brought this man
unto me, as one that perverteth the people; and, behold, I, having
examined him before you, have found no fault in this man touching
those things whereof ye accuse him. I will therefore chastise him,
and release him . . . And they cried out all at once, saying, Away with
this man, and release unto us Barabbas . . . Pilate therefore, willing
to release Jesus, spake again to them. But they cried, saying, Crucify
him, crucify him. And he said unto them the third time, Why, what
evil hath he done? I have found no cause of death in him: I will
therefore chastise him, and let him go. And they were instant with
loud voices, requiring that he might be crucified: and the voices of
them and of the chief priests prevailed.

When Pilate saw that he could prevail nothing, but that rather a
tumult was made, he took water, and washed his hands before the
multitude, saying, I am innocent of the blood of this just person:
see ye to it.

Luke 23:1-5, 13-24
John 19:17

And he bearing his cross went forth . . .

And the soldiers led him away into the hall . . . and they clothed him with purple, and platted a crown of thorns, and put it about his head, and began to salute him, Hail, King of the Jews! And they smote him on the head with a reed, and did spit upon him, and bowing their knees worshipped him. And when they had mocked him, they took off the purple from him, and put his own clothes on him, and led him out to crucify him.

And he bearing his cross went forth into a place called the place of a skull, which is called in the Hebrew Golgotha.

And there followed him a great company of people, and of women, which also bewailed and lamented him. But Jesus turning unto them said, Daughters of Jerusalem, weep not for me, but weep for yourselves, and for your children . . . And when they were come to the place, which is called calvary, there they crucified him, and the malefactors, one on the right hand, and the other on the left.

Then said Jesus, Father, forgive them; for they know not what they do. And they parted his raiment, and cast lots.

Mark 15:16-20
Matt. 27:24
Luke 23:26-34

Painting opposite
THE CARRYING OF THE CROSS
Joseph Maniscalco

The angel of the Lord descended from heaven, and came and rolled back the stone from the door, and sat upon it.

In the end of the sabbath, as it began to dawn toward the first day of the week, came Mary Magdalene and the other Mary to see the sepulchre. And, behold, there was a great earthquake, for the angel of the Lord descended from heaven, and came and rolled back the stone from the door, and sat upon it. His countenance was like lightning, and his raiment white as snow: And for fear of him the keepers did shake, and became as dead men. And the angel answered and said unto the women, Fear not ye: for I know that ye seek Jesus, which was crucified. He is not here: for he is risen, as he said. Come, see the place where the Lord lay. And go quickly, and tell his disciples that he is risen from the dead; and, behold, he goeth before you into Galilee; there shall ye see him: lo, I have told you. And they departed quickly from the sepulchre with fear and great joy; and did run to bring his disciples word.

Then the eleven disciples went away into Galilee, into a mountain where Jesus had appointed them. And when they saw him, they worshipped him: but some doubted. And Jesus came and spake unto them, saying, All power is given unto me in heaven and in earth.

Go ye therefore, and teach all nations, baptizing them in the name of the Father, and of the Son, and of the Holy Ghost: Teaching them to observe all things whatsoever I have commanded to you: and, lo, I am with you always, even unto the end of the world. Amen.

Matt. 28:1-8, 16-20

God's Corner

Gertrude M. Puelicher

Have you ever felt entrapped in a forest of branches so entwined that you could find no way out? The more frantically you flailed with your arms, the more closely did the branches enmesh, a buttress against which you were helpless. Suddenly, from high above you came the clear, sweet notes of a bird. The mesmerism that had enchained you was broken. You weren't alone, locked into an impenetrable woods; there was a way out, and you found it.

The dawning of Easter in our consciousness is like the bird call in its effect upon anxiety or fear. The recognition of Easter as a powerful factor in solving what seem like indissoluble problems can open up a new way of life. There are those to whom Easter spells fashion. There are those to whom Easter is an exciting search for colored eggs in the overwhelming social status of the White House lawn. There are those to whom Easter is just another reading of the Sunday comics.

However, there are also those to whom Easter is a day of joyous thanksgiving—a conscious awareness of good opening up for a world that recognizes the importance of stepping out of a tomb of dark humanhood into the warmth and sunlight of spiritual freedom.

Easter lilies and triumphant organ music carry an emotional impact that is dissipated when one leaves an Easter service and steps back into the mundane world of Easter ham and its gourmet accompaniments. The real impact of this day lies in an inner gratitude for the healing of a loved one, the solving of a problem that needed the light of Easter faith, the unfoldment within ourselves of an illumined meaning to the Easter message, "Christ is risen."

And Christ is risen within each of us when we accept the truth, "There is a spirit in man—." The fantastic statement was made recently that Christianity is on the way out. Christ on the way out? Utterly incredible! So long as there is one individual in the universe who recognizes the presence of the Christ within himself, his Christ consciousness will arouse the Christ dormant within those around him and Christianity will survive. Easter symbolizes the rebirth of the Christ consciousness, a rebirth that is eternal.

Just as the legendary phoenix arose anew out of the ashes of the old, let us accept the inspiration of the Easter message and welcome each new day with the joyous acknowledgment that Christ is risen as we leave behind us more and more humanhood and put on more and more of the Christ.

Song of Easter

Easter lilies! Can you hear
What they whisper, low and clear?
In dewy fragrance they unfold
Their splendor sweet, their snow and gold.
Every beauty-breathing bell,
News of heaven has to tell.
Listen to their mystic voice,
Hear, O mortal, and rejoice!
Hark, their soft and heavenly chime!
Christ is risen for all time!

Celia Thaxter

Photo opposite
Alpha Photo Associates

Pototschnik·

Loveliest of Trees

Loveliest of trees, the cherry now
Is hung with bloom along the bough,
And stands about the woodland ride
Wearing white for Eastertide.

Now, of my threescore years and ten,
Twenty will not come again,
And take from seventy springs a score,
It only leaves me fifty more.

And since to look at things in bloom
Fifty springs are little room,
About the woodlands I will go
To see the cherry hung with snow.

A. E. Housman

Our Little Girl

There's a song in her heart
   That I hope she may sing
All the days of her years
   As she does in their spring.

She's as sweet as a flower,
   As dainty and gay.
She will do something charming
   Then laugh it away.

Her brown eyes are merry
   And sparkling with fun
Except when she learns
   Of an injustice done.

Ah, then they spit fire,
   I wish you could see,
For it's just as they used to do
   When she was three.

She gives of herself,
   And who can give more.
Isn't that the one thing
   We're all longing for?

May the song in her heart
   And the joy that she gives
Be returned in full measure
   As long as she lives.

Alice B. Dorland

Dear little girl with stars in your eyes,
Touched by the radiance of golden skies;

Dear little girl with light in your hair,
Catching the colors that rainbows wear;

Dear little girl, stay as sweet as you are,
Hold fast to your dreams and reach for a star!

Fleta Bruer Gonso

The Willow Cats

They call them pussy willows
    But there's no cat to see,
Except the little furry toes
    That stick out on the tree.

I think that very long ago,
    When I was just born new,
There must have been whole pussy cats
    Where just the toes stick through;

And every spring it worries me,
    I cannot ever find
Those willow cats that ran away
    And left their toes behind!

Margaret Widdemer

From LITTLE GIRL AND BOY LAND by Margaret Widdemer, copyright, 1924, by Harcourt Brace Jovanovich, Inc.; renewed, 1952, by Margaret Widdemer Schauffler. Reprinted by permission of the publishers.

Pussy Willow Time

The pussy willows soft and sweet
    Are here again this spring;
What lovely overtures of joy
    To my own heart they bring.

They hint of spring; and every year
    Their age-old promise keep,
These silky catkins all curled up
    Like kittens fast asleep.

When stroked by sun and gentle breeze,
    It seems sometimes that I
Can hear them purr a friendly purr,
    Or just a little sigh.

It's spring! It's spring! I thrill to see
    The very sight of them.
These furry puffs of velvet plush,
    Wee kittens on a stem!

Georgia B. Adams

Bruce Coleman, Inc.

When you see a fuzzy bunny
That would be so nice to squeeze,

Hopping all around the shrubbery
Or beneath the orchard trees,

He may not be there for playing,
But in his happy way,

May be hiding candy eggs
For you to find on Easter Day!

George L. Ehrman

The Easter Bunny

Once upon an Easter, sunny,
Came a little frisky bunny
With his bit of fluffy cotton
Pasted where the spanks are gotten:

Curious little wiggly nose,
Pink and pretty as a rose;
Picked-up ears all satin lined,
Fur all clean and slick and shined;

Hopping hops and making tracks
In the garden; eating snacks
Of the early peas and beans,
Carrot tops and 'sparagus greens;

Left some samples of his trade
In the rosebush where he laid
Five red Easter eggs for me,
Sweeter than the honeybee.

Two he laid beside the door;
In the garden there were more.
One he laid among the crocus—
Then a bit of hocus-pocus—

In the rhubarb there were three.
All this makes it plain to see
That by manner of such habit
This must be the Easter rabbit.

Minnie Klemme

The Legendary Johnny Appleseed

Johnny Appleseed was born John Chapman in Leominster, Massachusetts, on September 26, 1774. His mother died while he was a child and his father was serving in the Revolutionary War. It is not known when he left home, but Chapman began his work as a missionary for the Church of the New Jerusalem as a young man. He then moved across the country ahead of the settlers, planting the apple seeds which he brought from the cider mills in western Pennsylvania. He maintained nurseries in Ohio for a few years and then went into Indiana, Missouri, Illinois, and some say even further west.

As he made his way across the wilderness, Johnny Appleseed paid little attention to his own needs and was more concerned with helping others. It has been said that he wore tattered clothes and a cooking pot for a hat. He helped pioneer families get established by purchasing food and other supplies for them with the money received from the sale of his trees. Chapman often acted as liaison between the Indians and the settlers, as he was friendly with both.

His exact travels are not known, but he made his last trip to Ohio, returning to Indiana where he died in 1845 at the age of seventy-one. His life of service and dedication to all has been immortalized in numerous books, poems and songs. John Chapman is best remembered as Johnny Appleseed—the man who forged his way through the wilderness scattering apple seeds, faith and love, everywhere he went.

H. Armstrong Roberts

This Little Boy

He puts his tiny hand in mine
    And holds on, oh, so tight;
His big blue eyes, with lashes soft,
    Are twinkling in the light.

He toddles by with baby steps
    That never seem to stop,
He bangs on all my pans and climbs
    A chair, right to the top.

He brings me tulips from the yard:
    And yellow "dandy-lines,"
Yet who's received such a bouquet
    As from this son of mine?

Each night I tuck him into bed
    And he throws me a kiss;
That's when I really wonder how
    Do I deserve all this?

I know without this little boy,
    So trying, yet so sweet,
My home would be an empty house;
    My life be incomplete.

Helen Townley

Easter Egg Customs Around the World

The association of eggs with Easter is ancient. Just when it developed is not known, but the egg is a symbol of the life force in many countries and in many religions. It represents the revival of the fertility of the earth. The return of spring meant more to our remote ancestors than it does to us, for it was a sure promise of creature comforts of which they had been deprived during the winter months, including pleasant weather and a greater variety of food.

ITALY—Italian families bake a special round cake for the holy day and decorate it with Easter eggs. On Easter Eve the Italians take their eggs to church where they are blessed by the priest. At the Easter feast next day, these eggs are put in the center of the table with everything else arranged around them. There are sometimes as many as two hundred, all of them brightly colored. Everyone who enters the house during the holiday is offered at least one egg, and no one may refuse this token of the Resurrection. The custom of paying visits on the afternoon of Easter Sunday is a popular one. Children look forward to it because at each place they are given Easter eggs and sweets.

GERMANY—The Easter bunny, beloved of our own children, is German in origin. The boys and girls place nests in their gardens so that the Easter rabbit may fill them with eggs. If the weather is unpleasant, he hides them in various places inside the house. There are several popular egg games which take place throughout Germany. Egg gathering is one of these. Eggs are placed at certain intervals along a racetrack. Children run down the line with baskets, each trying to gather the most eggs. In northwestern Germany, peasants hold contests to see who can devour the most eggs. A favorite decoration in Germany is the Easter egg tree. Decorated eggshells are suspended from a branch or small tree with loops of colored ribbon. The egg trees vary and some families also hang cakes or sweets, in the form of rabbits and lambs, from the tree's branches. Others place a nest of gifts beneath the tree. The Easter egg tree is then put in a prominent place for all to admire.

BULGARIA—Bulgarian families prefer red Easter eggs and always place the first decorated egg before the family icon as a symbol of the Resurrection. The farmers believe that if they sprinkle ashes around their chicken yards on Good Friday, eggs will be plentiful all year. It is also customary to exchange gifts of eggs and cakes on Passion Saturday.

GREECE—When friends or relatives meet on Easter day, one knocks a red egg against the egg of the other and utters the greeting, "Christ is risen." The other person replies, "Truly, He is risen." Then the eggs are exchanged. A food typical of the Greek Easter feast is called the Bread of Christ. It is a special round loaf of bread, marked with a Greek cross and decorated with red Easter eggs.

RUSSIA—Among White Russians it has long been a practice to give exquisitely decorated eggs as presents. Usually these are not real eggs, but some of them are of great value because of their extraordinary craftsmanship. Inside the eggs there are often tiny tableaus, scenes of Russia, or miniature paintings of royal personages. Another style of Easter eggs, the Ukrainian *pysanky*, are beautiful works of art. The name is derived from the Ukrainian verb, *pysaty*, which means "to write." The designs which decorate the eggs are drawn with a stylus dipped in beeswax. The *pysanky* vary in design from village to village, but certain motifs such as plants, animals and geometric patterns remain common throughout the Ukraine. No two eggs are ever alike.

UNITED STATES—Children of the United States enjoy many Easter customs, one of which is the annual egg-rolling contest on the White House lawn in Washington, D.C. This has taken place each Easter Monday since it began when Rutherford B. Hayes was president. The children roll their eggs downhill, and the egg which rolls the farthest without cracking wins. The boys and girls make up other egg games on their own. When they have rolled all the eggs they brought, they often roll down the hill themselves, laughing merrily all the way. The event is a memorable one, enjoyed by young and old alike.

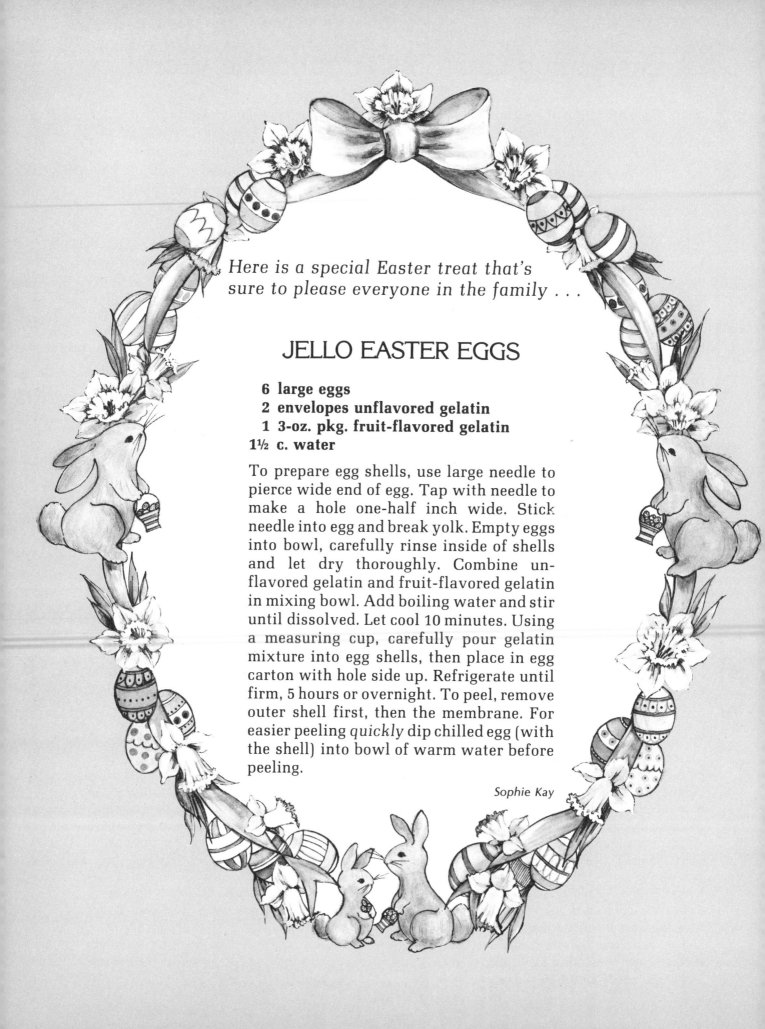

Here is a special Easter treat that's sure to please everyone in the family . . .

JELLO EASTER EGGS

6 large eggs
2 envelopes unflavored gelatin
1 3-oz. pkg. fruit-flavored gelatin
1½ c. water

To prepare egg shells, use large needle to pierce wide end of egg. Tap with needle to make a hole one-half inch wide. Stick needle into egg and break yolk. Empty eggs into bowl, carefully rinse inside of shells and let dry thoroughly. Combine unflavored gelatin and fruit-flavored gelatin in mixing bowl. Add boiling water and stir until dissolved. Let cool 10 minutes. Using a measuring cup, carefully pour gelatin mixture into egg shells, then place in egg carton with hole side up. Refrigerate until firm, 5 hours or overnight. To peel, remove outer shell first, then the membrane. For easier peeling *quickly* dip chilled egg (with the shell) into bowl of warm water before peeling.

Sophie Kay

The Lamb

Little lamb, who made thee?
Dost thou know who made thee,
Gave thee life and bade thee feed
By the stream and o'er the mead;
Gave thee clothing of delight,
Softest clothing, woolly, bright;
Gave thee such a tender voice,
Making all the vales rejoice?
    Little lamb, who made thee?
    Dost thou know who made thee?

Little lamb, I'll tell thee;
Little lamb, I'll tell thee.
He is called by thy name,
For He calls himself a Lamb;
He is meek and He is mild,
He became a little child.
I a child and thou a lamb,
We are called by His name.
    Little lamb, God bless thee!
    Little lamb, God bless thee!

William Blake

With Special Grace

Cathedral bells ring out today
With joyous Easter strain;
And everywhere, each hymn and prayer
Resound His praise again.

The promise of an earth renewed
Has happened overnight.
The woods are seen in vibrant green and
Lilies wear pure white.

Little creatures venture out—
Wee bunnies, frisky squirrel—
Each small child begs to hunt for eggs
In this glad springtime world.

Easter dinner, family style,
Is served with special grace.
There must be tons of hotcross buns
And ham at every place.

This special day, these moments shared,
The quiet way spring came
Proclaim rebirth. Let all the earth
Sing praises to His name!

Brenda Leigh

Easter 1912

When I was a child, I lived in a house that was divided into a home and a store. My favorite place in the store was the candy corner. The west front window and a glass counter next to it was given over completely to displaying candy. The candy corner ushered in all holidays of the year.

Next to Christmas, my favorite holiday was Easter and our candy corner helped to make it so. The candy window was full of pink and white and chocolate marshmallow rabbits and eggs. Soft yellow, sugary chicks lay in neat rows between the solid milk chocolate rabbits, elegant in their shiny gold and silver foil wrappers. Tiny tin frying pans containing creamy, candy sunny-side-up fried eggs and other Easter novelties, all at a penny each added to the charm of the display.

The shiny glass candy counter attracted the older customers. Pretty dishes of pastel bon-bons, maple and chocolate fudge, coated nuts, caramels and chocolate creams—all selling for a penny a piece made a mouth-watering display. Tall jars of jelly beans and stick candy decorated the back shelves of the candy corner along with the fancy be-ribboned boxes of gift candy.

Because there were so many sweets around to tempt young appetites, we children were allowed only small amounts occasionally. However, both my little sister and I had a "sweet box" which held many forbidden goodies to munch when we were playing up in our room—away from the grown-ups. This "sweet box" was always hidden in the farthest corner of our clothes closet.

"What's all this?" demanded Mama one day as she cleaned the shelves in the children's clothes closet.
"It's my sweet box," I confessed, grabbing my treasure off the trash heap.

"Throw it out," Mama ordered mercilessly. "We'll have bugs and moths all over the place. The clothes closet is no place for food, especially for sweet, sticky stuff like this!"

We should have known better than to try to hide anything those days before Easter. Our house was always thoroughly scrubbed and cleaned to make ready for the holiday. Nothing was safe from broom and scrub brush and Mama's eagle eye—especially the one in the back of her head. She always seemed to know when we got into mischief, even when her back was turned.

"Alleluia, alleluia! Let the loud hosannas ring!" Those hosannas were loud and thrilling even at daybreak on very cold Easter mornings. Our Easter always started with the Sunrise Service. The long, cold trek home was full of happy anticipation; for the Easter basket hunt began the minute we got home. I shall never forget the year that Toby, our shaggy shepherd dog, found our baskets first. He must have begun his hunt as soon as we left for the service that morning. Even our disappointment couldn't cover up the amusing sight Toby made lying guiltily and quietly in the middle of the mess he had made of all those lovely Easter nests—sick as a dog!

Breakfast on Easter morning was a meal to remember. Usually, some of our cousins, aunts and uncles came along home with us. The Easter hunt went on while Mama was busy frying sausages and scrambling eggs. The table was full of baked goodies Mama had made the day before. As we all joined hands at the table, Papa led the grace, asking God's blessing and a fervent wish for everyone's health and happiness, and this day instead of the usual "Amen", we all shouted "Alleluia!"

Catherine Otten

A Prayer in Spring

Oh, give us pleasure in the flowers today;
And give us not to think so far away
As the uncertain harvest; keep us here
All simply in the springing of the year.

Oh, give us pleasure in the orchard white,
Like nothing else by day, like ghosts by night;
And make us happy in the happy bees,
The swarm dilating round the perfect trees.

And make us happy in the darting bird
That suddenly above the bees is heard,
The meteor that thrusts in with needle bill,
And off a blossom in mid-air stands still.

For this is love and nothing else is love,
The which it is reserved for God above
To sanctify to what far ends He will,
But which it only needs that we fulfill.

Robert Frost

"All Hail the Power"

"All hail the power of Jesus' name,"
The churches and cathedrals ring
With the majesty of this hymn. The choirs
Lift joyous voices as they sing:
"Bring forth the royal diadem,"
And the music of this clear command
Can all but bring before our eyes
The crown, the quick obeying hand.

And we, this Easter morning hour,
The wonder day of all earth's days,
Should crown Him with the jeweled crown
Of adoration and of praise.
He is the blessed risen Christ
Who one far day was left for dead;
But now alive for evermore.
He is truly risen as He said.
His promise of immortality
To those who trust, remains the same;
The whole wide world should shout His praise:
"All hail the power of Jesus' name."

Grace Noll Crowell

Forever Spring

I wish it were forever spring
    Never the summer or the fall,
But larks forever on the wing
    And mating birds that croon and call
Each other in the scented dawn
    While yet the dew is on the lawn.

I wish that it could always be
    Just like today—the field and flower
Could keep the freshness of today
    And hold the beauty of this hour
Like precious wine in crystal bowls,
    To quench the thirst of weary souls.

I know it could not be—I know
    The blossoms on the apple bough
Must wither to produce the fruit;
    And all this shining beauty now
Must pass like moons upon a lake,
    Unmindful of the toll they take.

But still I wish that Spring could stay,
Forever as it is today.

                                Edna Jaques

Now 'tis the season of the bird and the bee;
It's spring and, like nature, my spirit runs free.

Judy M. Lowman

Coming in Neighborly Ideals—

A special feature story on hand fans . . . an interesting look at the legendary "Buffalo Bill" —William J. Cody . . . the beloved poem, "The House by the Side of the Road," by Sam Walter Foss . . . a reminiscent look at "Box Supper Socials" . . . plus poetry and pictures reflecting the beauty of early summer and the close-knit feeling between neighbors and friends.

ACKNOWLEDGMENTS

OUR LITTLE GIRL (original title: DOROTHEA) by Alice B. Dorland. From ROAMING THE WIND, Copyright © 1955 by Alice B. Dorland. Used with permission of Dorothea Knowles. THROUGH THE GATEWAY OF THE SPRINGTIME . . . (two verses from her poem: GATEWAY TO SPRING) by Vera Hardman. From HAPPY MOMENTS by Vera Ramsdell Hardman. Copyright © 1972 by Vera Ramsdell Hardman. Published by Dorrance & Company. IT MUST BE SPRING by James J. Metcalfe. Copyrighted. Courtesy Field Enterprises, Inc. HAVE YOU EVER FELT ENTRAPPED . . . by Gertrude M. Puelicher. From EXCLUSIVELY YOURS, April 1977. Used with permission of the author.

Additional photo credits: Inside front cover, H. Armstrong Roberts. Inside back cover, Cape Cod, Massachusetts, Fred M. Dole.

Share The Beauty & Inspiration Of IDEALS Magazine . . . A Mother's Day Gift That Will Be Cherished The Entire Year

Here is the story of the real America, the good-news stories of down-to-earth Americans and the solid ideas and ideals they live by. Each issue of IDEALS includes...

Every bimonthly issue of IDEALS will bring surprises and stories they'll want to save . . . each time reminding them of your thoughtfulness.

We are so sure you and your gift recipients will feel this way about IDEALS that we proudly extend to every new subscriber our personal

MONEY BACK GUARANTEE

...in country, home and the American way ... beautiful pages of IDEALS—enter your ...oday. You needn't send any money now ... Simply mark the proper area on the ...k or postage-paid order card and we'll bill...

SUBSCRIPTION PLANS

...issues as published $10.00
...$5.00 under the single copy rate.)

...2 issues as published....................$17.00
...513.00 under the single copy rate.)

...18 issues as published $24.00
...521.00 under the single copy rate.)

...issues as published ....$ 7.50
...$2.50 under the single copy rate.)

...AS YOU READ PLAN

...ou-Read Plan: 1. Send no money now. ...ent issue, or any title you designate, by ...h an invoice and return envelope. ...y return mail. 4. The next issue will ...ally; you needn't reorder each time. If ...el your pay-as-you-read subscription, ...three weeks before publication date.

IDEALS ...BLICATION SCHEDULE

....	Jan.
....	Mar.
....	May
....	July
...ls	Sept.
....	Nov.

"Bound To Be Beautiful" IDEALS BINDER

As rich looking as the six issues it holds with metal rods that eliminate punching. Stiff royal blue leather-cloth cover, embossed in gold. Yours for only $4.00. Hardcover 8½ x 11 inches.

EVEN BACK THEN . . .

Mom's Concern For The Family Filled Many Anxious Hours With A Special Kind of Love and Inspiration

Now Provide Her With Many Hours Of Rewarding Reading Pleasure With The Special Kind Of Beauty And Inspiration Contained in

ideals

SPECIAL MOTHER'S DAY GIFT OFFER

Enter your own or FIRST 1-year (6 issues) Gift Subscription to IDEALS at the regular $10.00 price (a $5.00 SAVINGS under the single copy rate) and enter 1-4 ADDITIONAL Gift Subscriptions for Mother and friends for just $9.00 EACH—SAVE $6.00 UNDER THE SINGLE COPY RATE on each additional subscription entered.

Details On Reverse Side

Gift Name_____

Address _____

City_____

State _____ Zip _____

Sign Gift Card From: _____

Gift Name_____

Address _____

City_____

State _____ Zip _____

Sign Gift Card From: _____

SAVE $6⁰⁰

UNDER THE SINGLE COPY PRICE ON THE SECOND, THIRD, FORTH & FIFTH 1-YEAR SUBSCRIPTIONS

My Name_____

Address _____

City_____

State _____ Zip _____

☐ **CHECK** here if this your **RENEWAL**

☐ PAYMENT ENCLOSED

☐ BILL ME

New Gift Books That Mother Will Enjoy Receiving And Sharing With Loved Ones

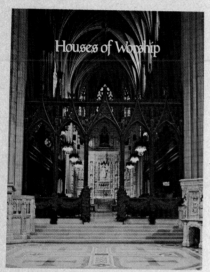
Houses of Worship

Cheerful Thoughts at Dawn
Alva F. Pingel, Jr.

Especially for Mother

THE GLORY OF EASTER

Messages of Hope

Happy Valentine's Day

Let's Have a Party!
Easy and Easy Decorating Ideas to Give Your Parties That Personal Touch

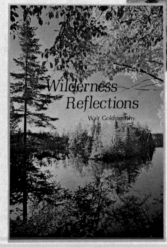
Wilderness Reflections
Walt Goldsworthy

Happy Birthday

Once Upon a Rhyme

Down Easter Bunny Lane

Naturally Nutritious, Naturally Delicious
by Donna M. Paananen

HOUSES OF WORSHIP — Glorious full color photos and inspiring prose allow you to visit some of America's most beautiful and historic churches and houses of worship. Pass through the ornately decorated archways of those built by noted 19th and 20th century architects . . . the quaint little church where George and Martha Washington were married . . . and the stately old church that played such a major role in the start of the Boston Tea Party. You and friends will marvel at these lovely structures and wonder at the tranquil beauty presented in their design, historical significance and breathtaking interiors. Hardcover — 8½" x 11" — 80 Pages — $3.95

CHEERFUL THOUGHTS AT DAWN — Here's a delightful pocket-sized gift book which is sure to make every day a little nicer for you and a friend. It's filled with light, cheerful, optimistic messages and is illustrated with charming black and white photos. Each message has a special, memorable meaning all its own. They help to re-enforce our beliefs in the good that exists in today's world and instill faith for even better tomorrows. As a gift, it's the perfect way to add a special bit of sunshine into a friend's life. Softcover — 4⅛" x 7" — 80 Pages — $1.50

ESPECIALLY FOR MOTHER — Oftentimes we forget to tell Mom just how much she really means to us. This specially designed gift book says it all. Sparkling color photos movingly reflect the many rewarding moments in a Mother's life while tender verse and prose convey your most heartfelt pledges of love and devotion to her. Make Mother's Day or any day personally hers with this touching token of love designed, "Especially For Mother." And don't forget all those other very special Moms on your list. Deluxe Puffed Cover — 5⅝" x 7½" — 40 Pages — $2.50

THE GLORY OF EASTER — Nature's colorful blossoming into springtime sets the stage for this captivating presentation of the customs, stories, religious significance, symbols and music that inspiringly reflects the many uplifting messages of Easter. You and those you remember with a thoughtful gift copy will travel to various parts of the world in celebration of this most glorious of holidays by means of lifelike photography, masterful art reproductions and inspired poetry and prose. Hardcover — 8½" x 11" — 80 Pages — Only $3.95

MESSAGES OF HOPE — Hope . . . the virtue by which a multitude of tomorrows have been made of . . . now is expressed in the most beautiful of poetic fashions. Coupled with full color pictures of some of nature's most breathtaking splendor, a tranquilizing tempo of heartwarming verse provides comforting thoughts of hope to nourish the heart and soul. For those many times one needs encouragement . . . for those many tomorrows yet to come. Deluxe Puffed Cover — 5⅝" x 7½" — 40 Pages — $2.50

LET'S HAVE A PARTY — features the most "unique" in decorating ideas and creative planning tips for all types of social gatherings. It includes step-by-step instructions and illustrations on how to make invitations, placemats and party favors. You'll learn how to easily sculpture vegetables into decorative floral bouquets and discover a number of delightful napkin folding ideas. It also features full color and black and white photos displaying novel ideas for parties with themes running from gay nineties get-togethers to celebrating Christmas in July. Softcover — 8½" x 11" — 64 Pages — **$2.75**

WILDERNESS REFLECTIONS — Open your heart to discovering how the many basic philosophies of life that we all share are so significantly paralleled by the many mysteries and magic of nature's ways. Walt Goldsworthy, in a number of short messages accented with charming art illustrations, inspiringly reflects upon the many precious lessons that can be inspired by the viewing of nature . . . how they can be applied to our daily living . . . and how important these lessons are in helping us to evaluate our goals for the future. Hardcover — 6" x 9" — 64 Pages — $2.95

HAPPY BIRTHDAY — is an especially wonderful way to tell a very special friend or relative that your thoughts are with them now and throughout the year. Beautiful color pictures and bright sparkling artwork help to illustrate what is in your heart as poetic expressions of friendship and love sincerely reflect your wishes for finding every joy and gladness in the year that starts that day. Send it in place of the usual greeting card as a gift in itself. Softcover — 8½" x 11" — 32 Pages — Only $1.50

HAPPY VALENTINE'S DAY — expresses your sincerest wishes for the happiest of all Valentine's Days in a new and distinctive way. Colorful photography, sensitive verse, sentimental prose and decorative artwork is warmly blended together in a full 8½" x 11" format, making this both a special greeting and a delightful gift book, too. It's appropriate for all ages, yet becomes so very personal by your giving, that it will be treasured for a long, long time. Softcover — 32 Pages — Only $1.50

ONCE UPON A RHYME — "Those golden rhymes, the ones your Mother taught you, the ones your child or grandchild, should really learn to." This hardcover treasury of easy-to-read verse and enchanting artwork features many of the best-loved rhymes of all time and blends them with many new rhymes. Hey Diddle Diddle, Simple Simon, Old Mother Hubbard and Jack Sprat are just a few of the many included. It's a lasting gift, that next to his teddy bear, is sure to become one of your child's most loved possessions. Hardcover — 8½" x 11" — 80 Pages — $3.95

DOWN EASTER BUNNY LANE — is an enchanting collection of Eastertime stories and rhymes. One-color photographs of cute little bunnies, kittens and puppies — all dressed for the occasion — illustrate these entertaining holiday fantasies that children will love to read and reread. It's a charming "little book" perfect for the Easter Basket — ideal as a gift from Grandmother when she visits during the holiday. Softcover — 8½" x 11" — 32 Pages — Only $1.50

NATURALLY NUTRITIOUS COOKBOOK FROM IDEALS Easy-to-prepare recipes for all types of dishes are included in this color photo-illustrated guide into cooking and baking with natural foods. Create healthy and tantalizing taste treats for family and friends using whole wheat flour, honey, brown rice, wheat germ, old fashioned molasses and other wholesome foods, including many you can grow yourself. Also included are bits of poetry, helpful cooking hints and a pinch of artwork. Softcover — 8½" x 11" — 64 Pages — $2.25

To Mother

With Love

FROM MAMA'S KITCHEN—includes easy-to-prepare recipes for soups, breads, meats, desserts, etc, and also contains food for thought. Here's a warmly developed blend of collected recipes and their related memories . . . as author, Catherine Smith, looks back in time to her childhood days . . . the aroma of molasses cookies in the country air . . . the sights and sounds of mama's kitchen. Here's a unique combination of nostalgic prose and delicious recipes that's sure to be a welcomed gift and used throughout the year. Softcover—8½" x 11"—64 Pages—Only $2.25

MOTHER'S DAY WISHES TO YOU—is a tender collection of the most sincere thoughts for Mom, brimming with love and artistically portraying your wishes for a joyful day in poetry and picture. It's a delightful gift by itself . . . or it can be used as a colorful and moving greetings wish to accompany a larger gift. And "Mother's Day Wishes To You" is the ideal gift too, for the many Moms who have meaningfully touched your heart over the past years. Softcover—8½" x 11"—32 Pages—Only $1.50

ESPECIALLY FOR MOTHER—Oftentimes we forget to tell Mom just how much she really means to us. This specially designed gift book says it all. Sparkling color photos movingly reflect the many rewarding moments in a Mother's life while tender verse and prose convey your most heartfelt pledges of love and devotion to her. Make Mother's Day or any day personally hers with this touching token of love designed, "Especially For Mother." And don't forget all those other very special Moms on your list. Deluxe Puffed Cover-5⅝" x 7½"—40 Pages—Only $2.50

MOTHER'S DAY GREETING—It's as much as a card in size . . . as much as a card in price, but it contains 10 times the verse and pictures than the average greeting card. 20 pages of brilliant color photos, artwork and poetry express heart-warming sentiments for Mother in this unique greeting booklet that will be truly appreciated and proudly displayed. Send it in the mail, attach it to a present, or personally present it to Mom with a kiss. Softcover—5⅜" x 7¼"—20 Pages—Only 75¢

A MOTHER IS LOVE—All the love and compassion found within a Mother's heart, along with those thoughts you find difficult to express, can be found among the lovely pages of this beautiful keepsake collection of inspirational prose and poetry for and about Mothers. Colorfully illustrated throughout, word and picture combine to capture the hearts of Mothers of all ages. Hardcover—7" x 9⅞"—64 Pages—Only $3.75